MY GAIA

poetry & photography

Wayne Sides

Jeanie Thompson

7 points press

MY GAIA

ISBN: 979-8-9907816-9-6
Cover Image: Wayne Sides

The following poems first appeared in slightly different forms in these collections:

How To Enter the River: "At the Wheeler Wildlife Refuge," "How to Enter the River," and "Snowy Egrets Flying Before a Storm"

Litany for a Vanishing Landscape: "The Lyrical Trees" and "Snapshot in the Red Fields"

The Seasons Bear Us: "Mother Memory," "Picking Blackberries on the Walk to Colonnata," "Fragment with Border," and "Among Ancient Olive Trees"

7 Points Press is a non-commercial entity dedicated to promoting the arts in the Shoals area of Alabama.

sevenpointspress@gmail.com

To order:
https://www.lulu.com/shop/jeanie-thompson-and-wayne-sides/my-gaia/paperback/product-e7wm6dr.html?page=1&pageSize=4

$20.00

MY GAIA

poetry & photography

Wayne Sides

Jeanie Thompson

Table of Contents

Anne Sullivan Arrives in Alabama, 1888

an edge of dirt road
a dirt road bounding a field of cinquefoil
that tumbles,

red dirt powdering
feet moving west
a cage of limbs against
late sun pouring gold –

makes me want to flee, Helen,
why not?

the silent field, the ripple of road
like stripped-off ribbon

a field of tossing yellow cinquefoil
a heart that longs for silence –

where am I
at this moment without a cricket
or bird to name it summer,
Alabama?
                                        caught in sunlight
dropping to dusk –
turn to the field, turn back?

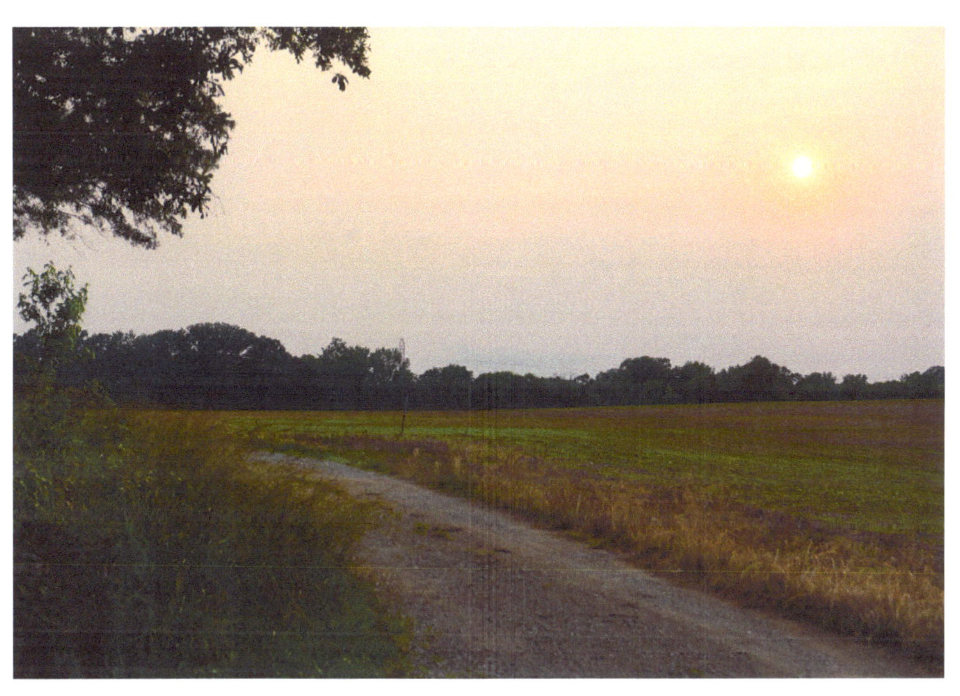

At the Wheeler Wildlife Refuge

Winter wheat, rabbit tobacco, sorghum
dried to a dark rattle.

Harvest of color in a dry wind.
Thorns low on the ground,

a network of warning.
Beyond this trail, cornfields

spread green in winter grass.
I stop walking to face the solid

stand of pines. I tilt my head back,
the air is sweet.

Closing my eyes I breathe again,
as deep as a blue-tick hound

when the scent floods past
rank and scared for life.

When I go, I'll take the four-lane
cutting through the backwater.

What tells me I'm alive –
impossible, useless to carry away.

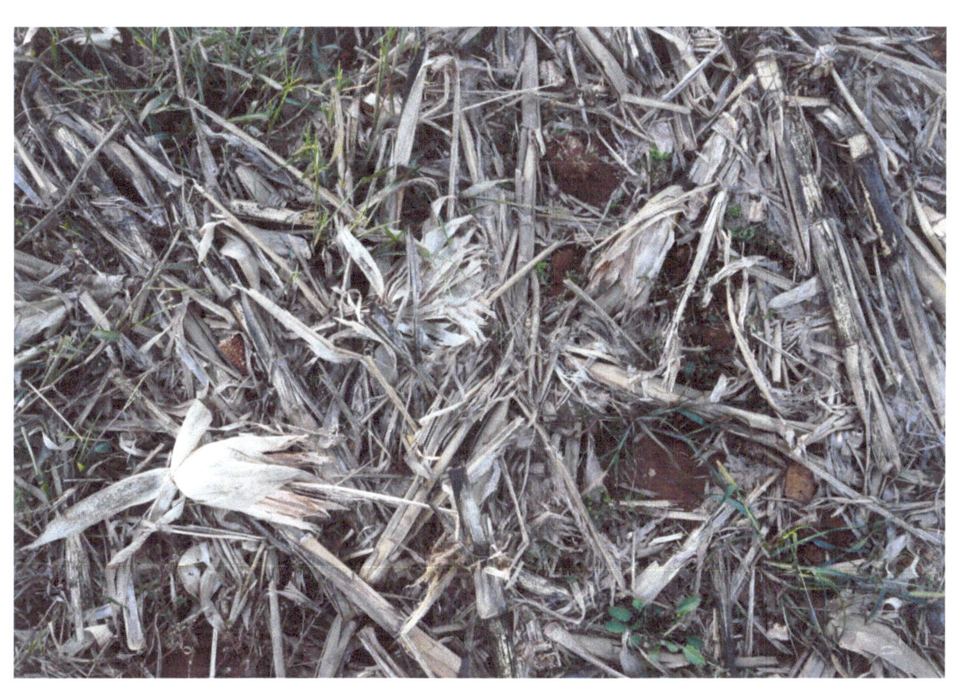

How To Enter The River

for Mickey Landry

The river sings for you now
in the green –
Trees bowing as you move past.

Beneath you, around you
the water is a muscle –
A heart of jewels spilled over rock.

The river sings for you now,
trees bowing as you move past.
This is how you enter the river.

I say
forget your hand on the paddle,
how your arm dips and pulls,
guides the board
to enter the water, unnoticed.

You keep your back turned
and move effortlessly
through the rapids,

sure of your skill, you feel
where the boat must go.
This is how you enter the river.

There is a sadness in your straight
impassive back
as if by turning from them

you will go on forever,
forever here
among lighted waters
flexing,
opening around you
in song.

This is how you enter the river –

And this is how you enter the river –

And this is how the river enters you –

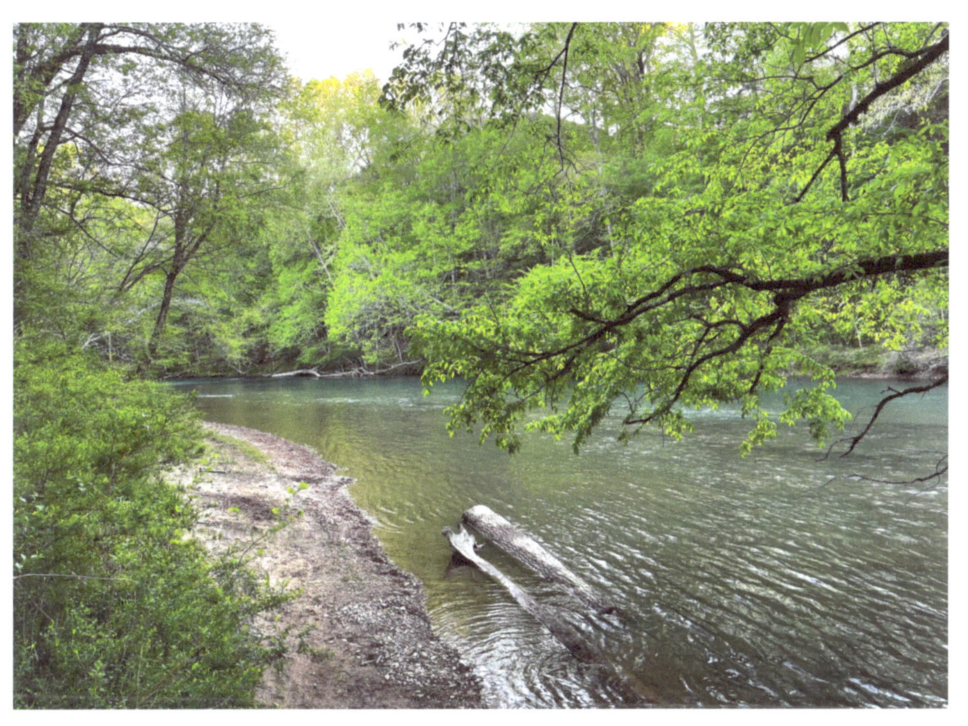

Snowy Egrets Flying Before a Storm

In the stillness just ahead of the storm
I saw snowy egrets lifting above a field.

Their bodies rose, a chorus
catching the current of the mightier air.

Their flock twisted and whipped,
a delicate net of feather, wing, and bone

that broke as the storm flew into them –
I felt the fear hold me,

I flew with it.

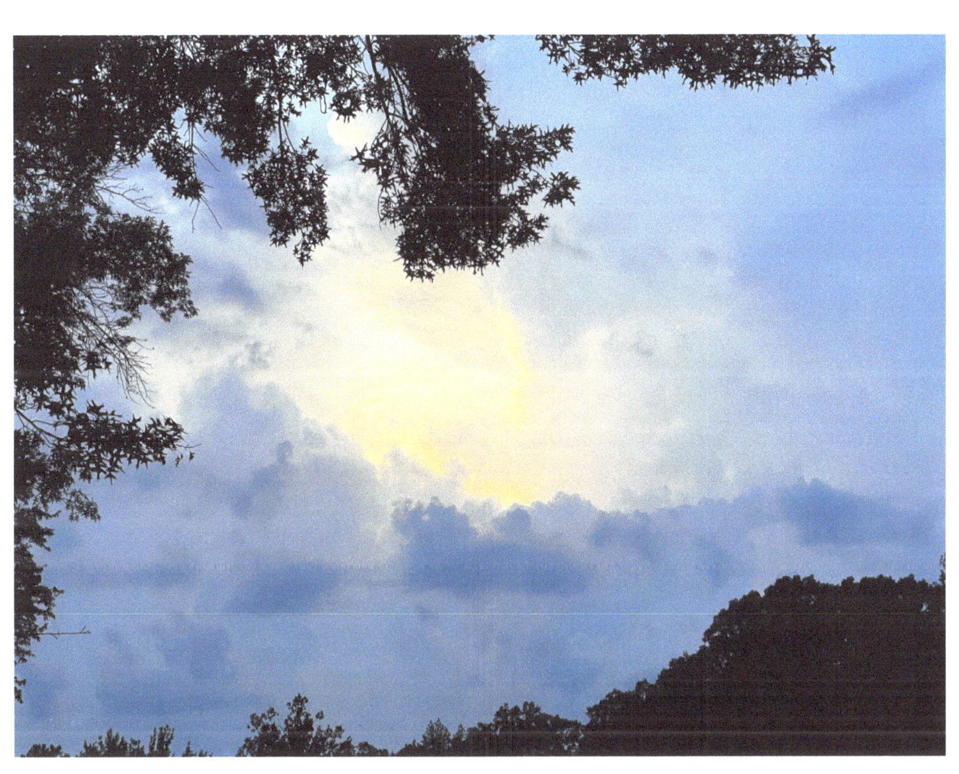

The Lyrical Trees

It's winter
and we've turned
once again
to the landscape

for some scrap of truth
to confound us,
to show us who we are.

The land is cold,
burrowed deep into itself.
A brown furze covers
the pastures

where cattle huddle against
one another
in bitter afternoon light.

Across the field,
around the deserted house,
over the trees,

the vines of summer
make a ghost network
holding fast for spring.

It's all set to pull us down,
into its slow heartbeat,
all but these three,

rising in twists
that dancers dream to imitate,

in love with this season –
when their beautiful, bare limbs,
their smooth bark

can sing and move upward
in the shattering air –
those lyrical trees –

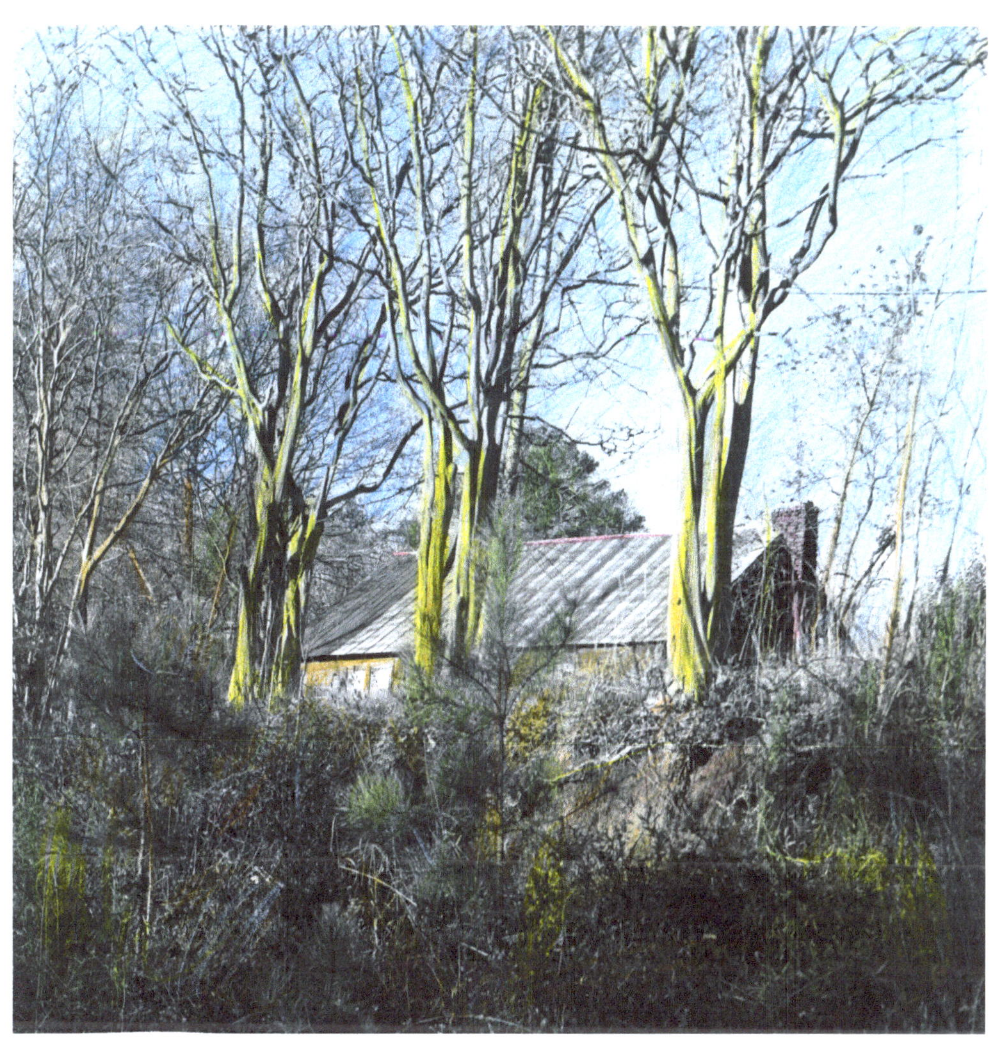

Snapshot in the Red Fields

Dirt cakes his boot soles
as he steps down from the machine
idling now in the field

The sun slants toward evening
and the smell of damp, just-turned earth
fills him so that he thinks he will burst with it

He must stop and look now, before the daylight leaves,
before the hawk spreads
its wings one last time, drops into a row
and disappears over the tree grove –
the machine coughs, a dirty cloud of diesel
plumes the air,
he sifts the earth through his fingers,

something he can't touch often enough,
impossible to explain to anyone
how the fields keep him alive,
and at this moment, when
the plow has turned the rows,
and the earth is open before him,
he would just as soon dive into it
and forget himself, – down, down into its depth
rather than lose it or know
that the season would not come again

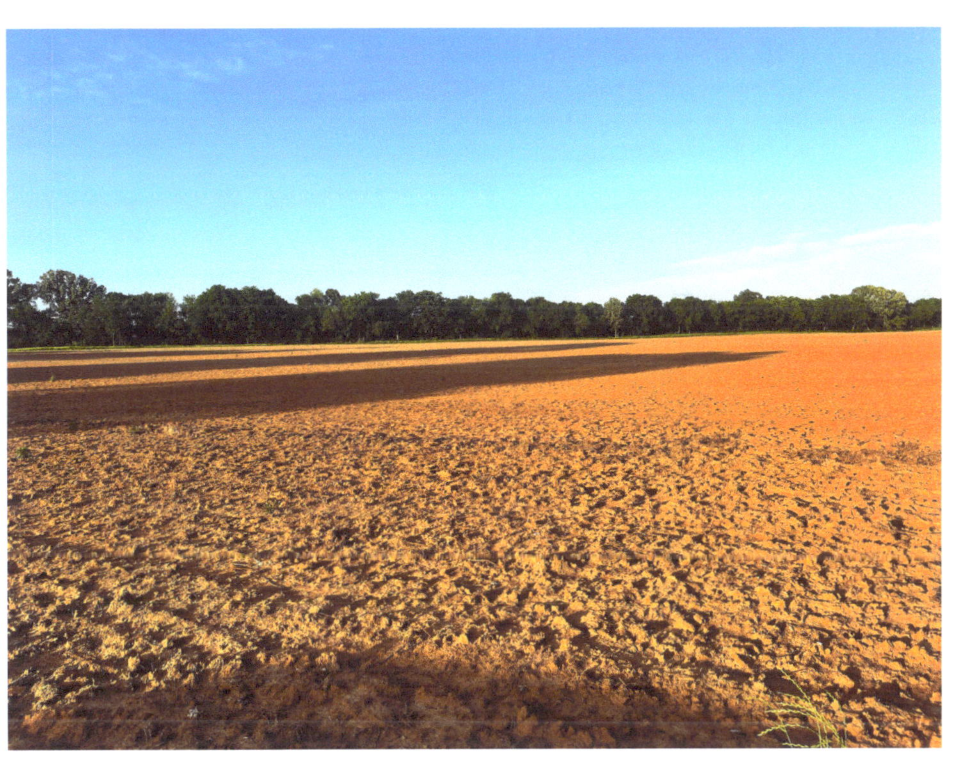

Mother Memory

at Shark's Tooth Creek / Greene County, Alabama

As I lead my son down the creek,
brown water swirling to our thighs,
I think of the Bahama's undulating blue
closing quietly over our heads.
Feet gripping the pebbly bed, we
breathe easily under a tree-canopy
holding the tropical heat at bay,
sifting our way through silt in search
of sharks' teeth from seventy million years ago.

I stop to cup a handful of sandy gravel
and spread it on my palm so he can
find the slender needle.
When I spread the pieces, he lifts
the ebony charm from smooth stones,
and I wonder what power takes shape
before this young boy's eyes.
Does the dorsal fin graze his calf?
Does he feel the terrible rush of water
sucking everything in? Can he know
that moment when life transmutes to other matter

like an ocean calming to creek water
where we stand, passing an ancient
creature's remains from hand to hand?

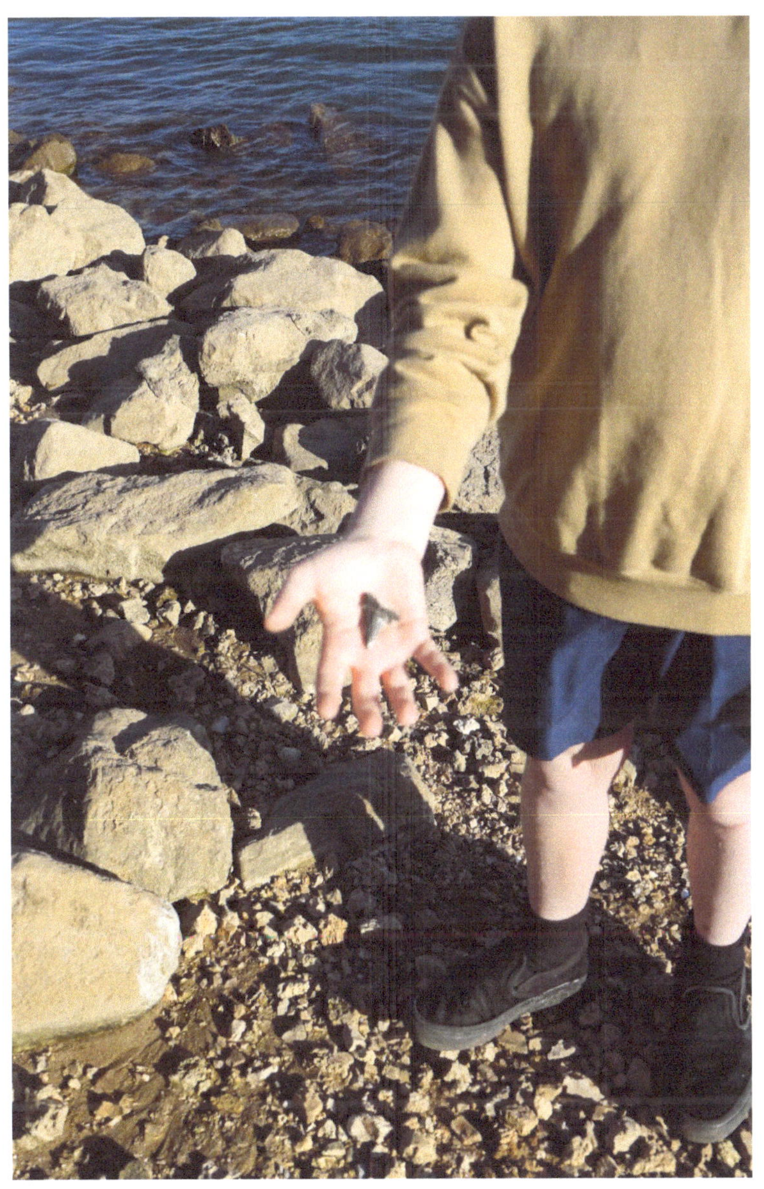

Picking Blackberries on the Walk to Colonnata

in the Apuan Alps, Tuscany, Italy

After the quarries, as we troop up the winding mountain road
        on our way to Colonnata, Daniele spots a treat
to share with us. He climbs the rock wall like
        a knowledgeable bear after fruit sweet as any summer.
Later we will see the crucifix from 1584,
        school of Michaelangelo.
Part of me had remained in the marble tomb of the cave
        at Carrara, where we learned how the blocks were cut,
and children splashed in puddles at the center of the mountain.
        Those cool floors and soaring walls had invited us to stay.
We felt their spirit, forgot the world outside.
        The sun glinted on marble toys and the world was still
crazy with war and death.
                                        But here at the moment of our walk
        to Colonnata, there were blackberries, sweet, staining
the fingers of our friend's hand as he said, "Here is a big one!"
        and offered the fruit to me.

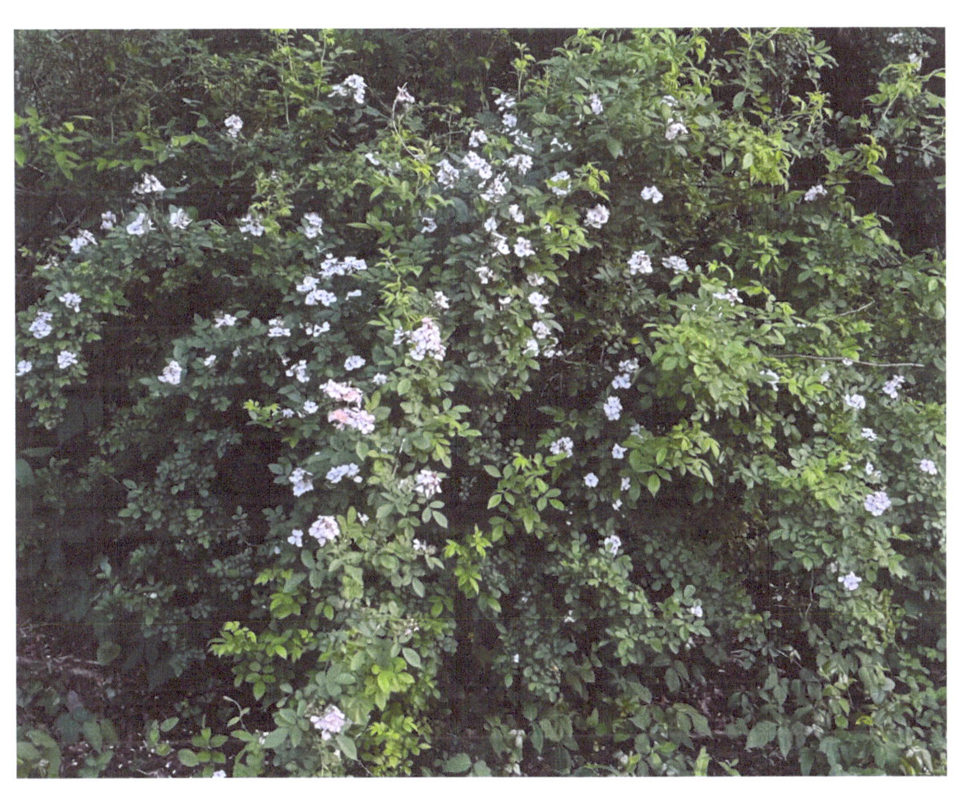

Fragment, with Border

What held me was the sky cut against the sea,
          blue abutted to azure-blue, horizon invisible,

a border to be crossed. Earlier, the plane had banked
          above Paris, ink-stained, the tower below, and those streets!

As close as I would get this time. Approaching Nice, the plane banked
          over the Mediterranean and held me like an audience of one,

harbors, little flags of ships, the pink-breasted dome
          of the Negresco bared to the sea.

When the wheels touched my world to yours, tongue
          against tongue, released, I tumbled in the language fragment.

That first night, we walked into the ancient city, and I knew home,
          crossed that border – no need to tell. Je voudrais,

je voudrais…I would like my language to meet yours,
          the way the hills sliced the shoreline, my feet

recognized the bruise of small stones, rosemary
          and lavender wafted around us, simple southern wildflowers,

a cold stream raced our hearts.
          In the dream that holds me, I step over a clear demarcation

into the city – ancient, rich, pungent, and dark –
          If I spoke of this,

would the dream break, fragile as a cup of memory?
          No one would hold me, no one knew,

I was made new and shattered, lost. Oh, familiar, alien landscape –
          tree, rock, cloud, water, bumble bee, human hand, kiss!

No one could hold me, no one knew. I wanted something –
          nothing. To be held. Released. On that shore, nowhere else.

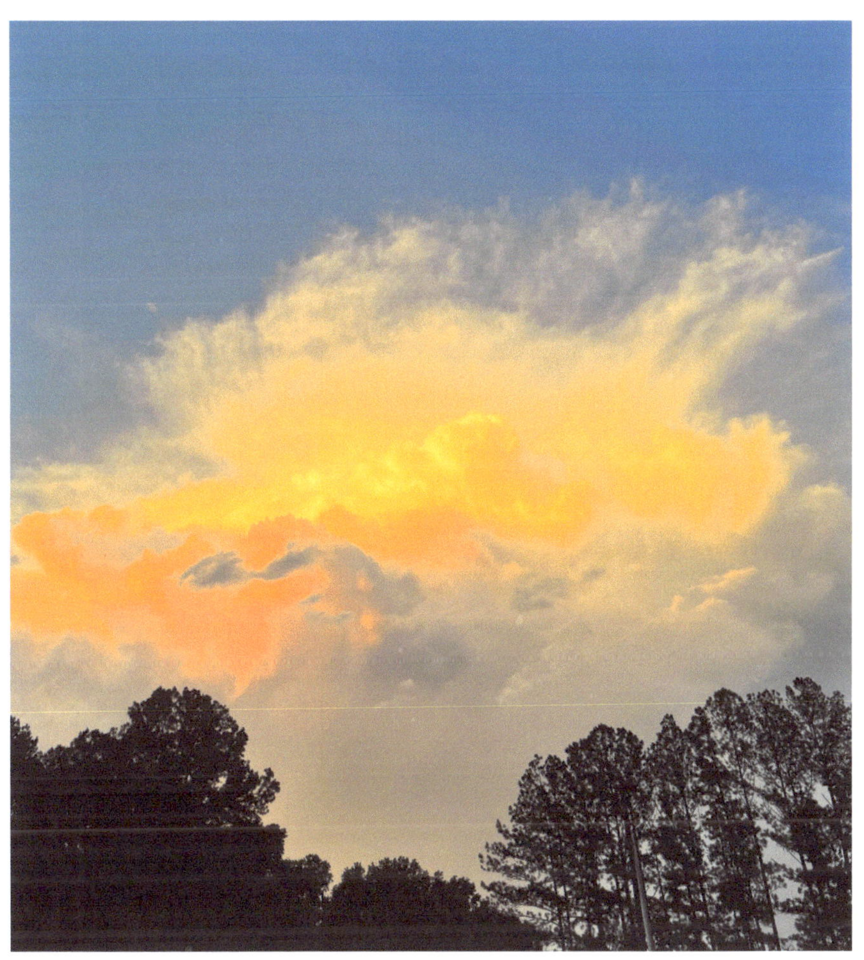

Among Ancient Olive Trees
for Wayne

When we climb the path to the medieval wall above Pietrasanta
    without knowing really where we are, we stumble into an olive grove.

Because we do not live where ancient walls are lit by floodlights at dusk,
    and benches wait where one can view the medieval tower, or the piazza

below where a wedding spills from the Duomo,
    the trees seem older and older as we walk among them,

writing and talking, photographing quietly
    As the day turns toward evening, I am afraid we are losing the light –

but you say, "The light gets better, not lost." The leaves silver further
    toward olive and the blue-grey trunks deepen their fingers to earth,

the shutter clicks over and over a steady hand tending roots and fruit-fall.
    We might wander here for years, children in a fairy tale,

hearts brimmed full of the deepening color, welcoming
    those who seek their presence past the call of home.

Companionable light enters the leaves, turns them dusky jade
    shimmering above us
                                        – and we confess we crave this,
an image stilled on paper, a refuge we enter
    for the silence.

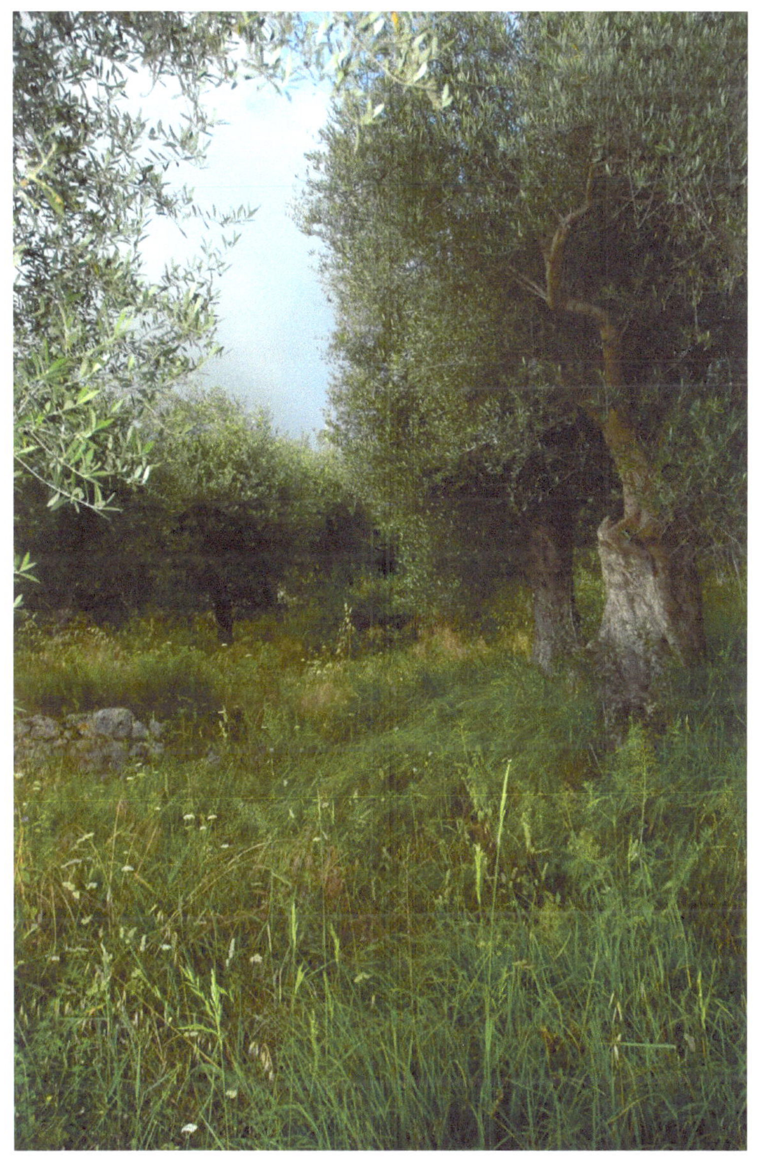

Cleome / 2025

Does poetry have to be our loudspeaker,
our psychotherapist, a substitute
for doing the hard work of getting people out to vote,
our personal platform? This is a serious question.

Maybe poetry is more like the cleome plant,
sprouting leaves that look like cannabis
so that you may think a stranger, or a playful friend,
has dropped seeds in your patio garden.
She builds a small ladder of non-potent leaves
in preparation for the announcement
of a flower. Beginning as small buds,
unassuming as snapdragons tinged pink,
            it hovers there
while tiny wire-like tendrils begin
to spoke out like a satellite
and claim the space around the flower.
It might float there and entice us
to touch and cup these tendrils,
like the nimbus of your child's hair around his singularly
amazing small skull.

My friend gave me one of these
for my journey home – to watch, to touch.
At first, I thought it had died in transit
but today it hangs in its tiny nimbus
surrounded by garden giants – flopped-over cannas
flattened by rain. The cleome is there
taking stock of her new surroundings,
orbiting herself, completely, happily
unaware of humans and weather.

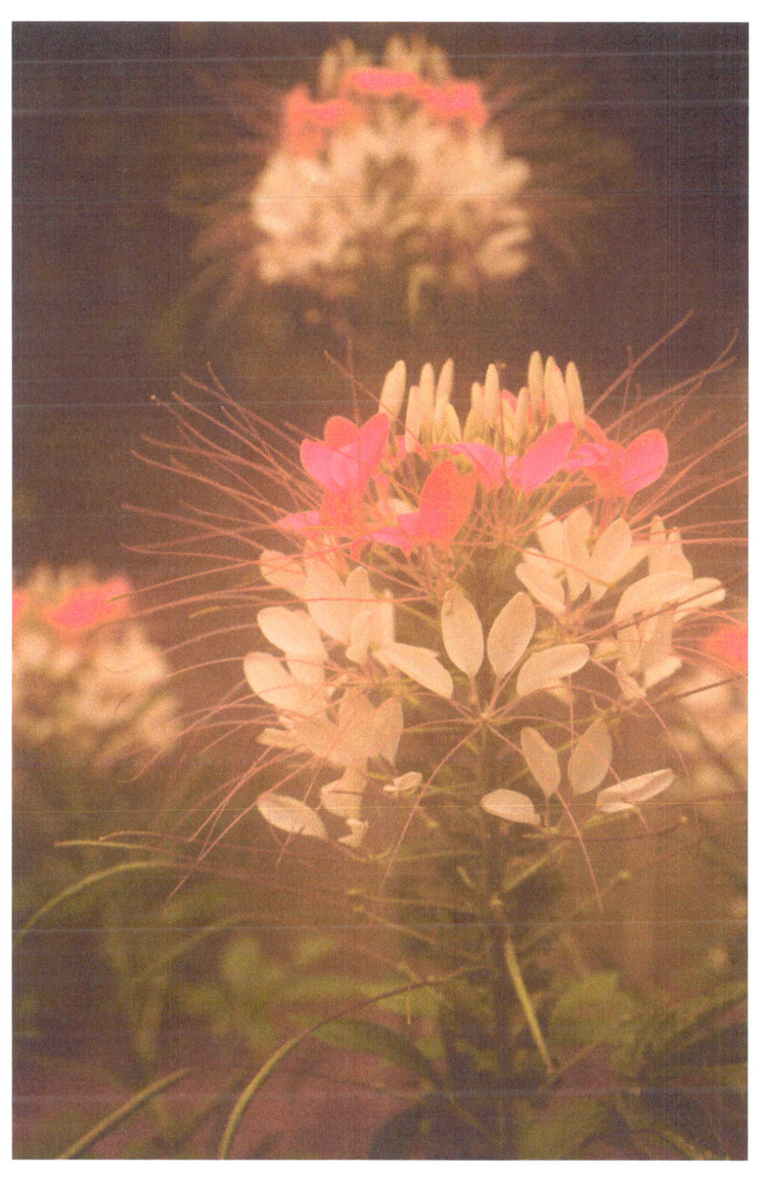

About the Artists

Wayne Sides is a native of Calhoun County, Alabama, and currently resides in Florence, Alabama. He received a B.A. degree in visual and performing arts from the University of Alabama New College in Tuscaloosa and earned a M.A. degree in photo image making/art from Pratt Institute in Brooklyn, NY. He worked as a lecturer and artist in residence with Southwest State University of Marshall, MN.; the New York Federation for the Arts; the Whitney Museum of American Arts; and the Alabama State Council of the Arts, among others. His work has been displayed internationally, including the OK Harris Gallery, Soho, NYC; A Palazzo Panichi Museum in Pietrasanta, Italy; and the Birmingham Civil Rights Museum in Birmingham, AL.

His photographs are published in several books including *Side Show, Litany for a Vanishing Landscape* (with poems by Jeanie Thompson), *White Knights, Silence and the Hammer, Human Traces, Gather Up Our Voices,* and *Interpreter.* Sides' photographs have also been used as cover art for the novels *The Ballad of Little River* by Paul Hemphill and *Goodbye to the Buttermilk Sky* by Julia Oliver. He created the book cover art for four poetry collections by Jeanie Thompson: *How to Enter the River, Witness, White for Harvest: New and Selected Poems,* and *The Myth of Water: Poems from the Life of Helen Keller.*

Sides is Professor Emeritus from the University of North Alabama and remains active in the Shoals area arts scene. He created a multi-media installation for *The Myth of Water* titled "I Wake from a Dream" that was on view at the Helen Keller Public Library in Tuscumbia from summer 2019 through fall 2020.

WayneSides.com

Jeanie Thompson is an Alabama native, an award-winning poet, teacher, and literary arts leader, who writes, teaches, and collaborates in her home state. She received her B.A. in English and M.F.A. in Creative Writing from the University of Alabama where she was founding editor of the literary journal *Black Warrior Review*. Her poetry collections include *How to Enter the River*, *Witness*, *White for Harvest: New and Collected Poems*, *The Seasons Bear Us*, and *The Myth of Water: Poems from the Life of Helen Keller*. With Jay Lamar, she edited *The Remembered Gate: Memoirs by Alabama Writers*. Her essays have appeared in various collections, including the 2024 volume *Old Enough: Southern Women Artists and Writers on Creativity and Aging* (UGA Press).

Thompson has been awarded two Alabama State Council on the Arts Fellowships for her work, and in 2024 she received the Albert Head Legacy Award from the Alabama State Council on the Arts for her work as founding director of the Alabama Writers' Forum (1993-2023). She remains passionate about literary arts programs for justice-involved youth.

In 2025 Thompson recorded selected poems from her poetry collections for which Grammy-winning producer and internationally known guitarist Larry Mitchell, of Opelika, Alabama, composed original music. Thompson's album, *The Myth of Water: Go Into Your Life,* will debut in fall 2025 on jeaniethompson.bandcamp.com.

jeaniethompson.com

www.ingramcontent.com/pod-product-compliance
Lightning Source LLC
LaVergne TN
LVHW052311100826
845147LV00006B/728
9798990781696